Nutrition

Minerals

by Janet Slingerland

FOCUS READERS

BEACON

www.focusreaders.com

Focus Readers is distributed by North Star Editions:
sales@northstareditions.com | 888-417-0195

Produced for Focus Readers by Red Line Editorial.

Photographs ©: Shutterstock Images, cover, 1, 4, 6, 8, 11, 12, 14–15, 16, 19, 20, 22, 25, 26, 29

Library of Congress Cataloging-in-Publication Data
Names: Slingerland, Janet, author.
Title: Minerals / by Janet Slingerland.
Description: Mendota Heights, MN: Focus Readers, [2025] | Series: Nutrition | Includes bibliographical references and index. | Audience: Grades 2-3
Identifiers: LCCN 2023053140 (print) | LCCN 2023053141 (ebook) | ISBN 9798889981831 (hardcover) | ISBN 9798889982395 (paperback) | ISBN 9798889983491 (pdf) | ISBN 9798889982951 (ebook)
Subjects: LCSH: Minerals in nutrition--Juvenile literature. | Food--Mineral content--Juvenile literature. | Nutrition--Juvenile literature.
Classification: LCC QP533 .S55 2025 (print) | LCC QP533 (ebook) | DDC 613.2/85--dc23/eng/20231222
LC record available at https://lccn.loc.gov/2023053140
LC ebook record available at https://lccn.loc.gov/2023053141

Printed in the United States of America
Mankato, MN
082024

About the Author

Janet Slingerland started out studying electrical engineering and programming computers. Now she writes. Janet has authored more than two dozen nonfiction books on a wide variety of topics, including animals and Wi-Fi.

Table of Contents

Chapter 1

A Good Breakfast

A boy grabs a jar out of the refrigerator. It has overnight oats inside. He mixed them the night before. The overnight oats are full of **nutrients** called minerals.

Oats are a type of grain. They contain many minerals.

Zinc is an important mineral for growing children. It is in meat, dairy, and seeds.

Oats and soy milk are the main **ingredients** in the boy's breakfast. The oats have lots of iron. The soy milk is a good source of calcium and copper.

The boy also stirs in raisins. They add several more minerals. One is zinc. Another is fluoride. Next, the boy sprinkles pumpkin seeds on top. They are a good source of potassium.

This easy breakfast tastes great. It's also good for the boy's body. It contains minerals to help him grow healthy and strong.

Chapter 2

Many Minerals

Minerals start as rocks or soil. They can also be in water. Plants absorb these minerals. Animals and people get the minerals from eating plants. They can also get minerals from eating animals.

Minerals make up about 4 percent of a person's body weight.

The body needs many different minerals to stay healthy. Calcium and phosphorus are two examples. These minerals help bones and teeth grow. Teeth need other minerals, too. Fluoride helps fight cavities.

Iron is another important mineral. The body uses iron to make hemoglobin. Hemoglobin is in red blood cells. It takes **oxygen** from the lungs. It moves the oxygen around the body.

Calcium is the most common mineral in the body. Milk is one good source.

Enzymes need minerals such as zinc and copper. Enzymes help the body breathe. They help digest food. They also help muscles and **nerves** work correctly.

Iodine is a mineral that is often found in seafood and dairy. It helps form certain hormones.

Hormones need minerals, too. Hormones are **chemicals** made in the body. They move around in blood. The body uses them to send messages to **tissues** and organs. One critical hormone is **insulin**. The body needs it to manage blood sugar. Chromium is a mineral that helps the body use insulin.

The body needs lots of different minerals. But it only needs tiny amounts of each one. Large doses can make a person sick.

People need 2 grams or less of each mineral per day.

A CLOSER LOOK

Electrolytes

Electrolytes are an important group of minerals. Electrolytes break down in water. Then, they become **ions**. They carry electrical signals around the body.

Nerves need electrolytes. That's because nerves use electricity to send signals to body parts. This is how they control movement. Electrolytes also help the body keep the correct levels of liquids. They help rebuild tissues, too.

Foods high in electrolytes include nuts, bananas, and spinach.

Chapter 3

Major and Trace Minerals

Minerals fall into two groups. People need larger amounts of major minerals. They need smaller amounts of trace minerals. Different foods have different types of minerals.

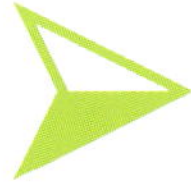

People may feel weak or sick when they do not get enough minerals.

There are seven major minerals. One of them is calcium. Beans are one source. Calcium is in dairy products, too. Milk and cheese are good sources. So is yogurt.

Protein-rich foods have a few major minerals. These foods include meats. They also include beans, nuts, and seeds. Protein-rich foods are good sources of sulfur. Many of these foods also have large amounts of phosphorus and magnesium.

Eggs, beef, and leafy vegetables are good sources of sulfur.

The other major minerals are potassium, sodium, and chloride. These come from a few different sources. Bananas have potassium. Sodium and chloride are in salt. Salt can be found in many foods.

Drinking water with added fluoride can protect teeth.

There are nine trace minerals. Chromium and fluoride are examples. So are iron and zinc.

Chromium is in whole grains and nuts. Fluoride is in fish and tea. Many cities also add fluoride to drinking water. Iron is found in meats and beans. Zinc comes from meat and tofu. It is also in seeds and beans. Other trace minerals are found in nuts and grains.

In the past, many people didn't get enough iodine. Now, this trace mineral is added to table salt.

Chapter 4

Healthy Plates

Humans need many different minerals. Some minerals are found in vegetables. Others are in nuts. And others are in grains. To get them all, it is best to eat many different kinds of foods.

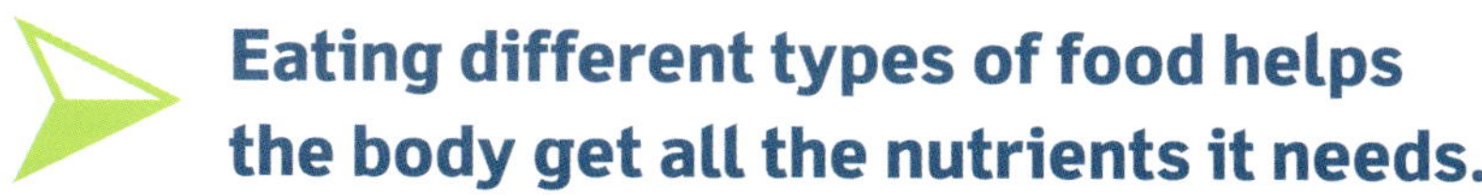

Eating different types of food helps the body get all the nutrients it needs.

A doctor may decide a person needs mineral supplements. But most people can get all the minerals they need from everyday meals.

However, some minerals are harder to get than others. Older people may not get enough calcium or potassium. Dairy products help people get calcium. Spinach can help with potassium. Other people may not get enough iron. Cooked soybeans or lentils can help.

Mineral supplements should not replace eating healthy foods.

Experts have suggestions for eating. Fruits and vegetables should cover half the plate. Having many different kinds and colors is best.

Making a weekly meal plan can help people get enough minerals.

One-quarter of the plate should be whole grains. Foods made with whole wheat and quinoa are healthy options. Oats and brown rice can be good sources, too.

The last quarter of the plate should be proteins. These include beans and nuts. Fish and **poultry** are also healthy choices.

Experts suggest eating several different healthy foods with each meal. That helps people get all the minerals they need.

Some pots and pans add minerals to food. Iron and copper are common examples.

FOCUS ON
Minerals

Write your answers on a separate piece of paper.

1. Write a sentence describing one way the body uses minerals.
2. What is your favorite source of calcium? What do you like about it?
3. Which word describes minerals that people need smaller amounts of?
   - A. major
   - B. trace
   - C. electrolytes
4. What might happen to a person who did not get enough fluoride?
   - A. She would get more cavities.
   - B. She would have stronger teeth.
   - C. She would not be able to use insulin.

5. What does **critical** mean in this book?

*One **critical** hormone is insulin. The body needs it to manage blood sugar.*

A. harmful or deadly
B. hidden or lost
C. important or needed

6. What does **supplements** mean in this book?

*A doctor may decide a person needs mineral **supplements**. But most people can get all the minerals they need from everyday meals.*

A. things that are added to improve health
B. things that are taken away to improve health
C. things that are not possible to eat

Answer key on page 32.

Glossary

chemicals
Specific kinds of matter. Some chemicals can be harmful, and some can be helpful.

ingredients
Foods that are mixed together to make a meal.

insulin
A hormone that controls how the body uses sugars.

ions
Atoms or groups of atoms that carry an electric charge.

nerves
Long, thin fibers that carry information between the brain and other parts of the body.

nutrients
Substances that living things need to stay strong and healthy.

oxygen
A gas in the air that humans and animals need to breathe to survive.

poultry
Birds including chickens, turkeys, and ducks.

tissues
Groups of similar cells in a plant or animal that have a certain job or function.

To Learn More

BOOKS

Davis, C. M. *Minerals as Necessary Nutrients*. Minneapolis: Abdo Publishing, 2023.

LaPierre, Yvette. *Your Body on Salt*. Minneapolis: Abdo Publishing, 2020.

Rebman, Nick. *Earth-Friendly Eating*. Mendota Heights, MN: Focus Readers, 2022.

NOTE TO EDUCATORS

Visit **www.focusreaders.com** to find lesson plans, activities, links, and other resources related to this title.

Index

Answer Key: 1. Answers will vary; **2.** Answers will vary; **3.** B; **4.** A; **5.** C; **6.** A